CONTENTS

CHAPTER 1 - WHY DO WE WORK?

CHAPTER 2 - IDENTIFYING YOUR POTENTIAL

CHAPTER 3 - MARKETING YOURSELF

CHAPTER 4 - THE INTERVIEW

CHAPTER 5 - MAINTAINING THE PASSION

Over the past few years I have spent a lot of my time having appreciative conversations with people in the work environment. The CPA (Career Path Appreciation) process is an Appreciative Conversation that explores the nature of work that individuals enjoy and that provides them with a sense of flow and confidence in their day to day activities. One of the questions I often ask during the conversation is: "What is the main purpose of the work you do?" and after exploring purpose I then ask them if they enjoy their work? Many people respond with - "I love my job". Some however, hesitate at this point, not sure what to say. They often mention the nature of their work, stress or people issues as the main source of their sense of discomfort at work I then explore the highs and lows of their careers and we look at times when they felt "In-Flow" at work and times when they felt either "Overstretched" or "Underutilised" at work. Usually, the hesitation on the previous question then becomes clearer. Times when we are "In-flow" are usually the happiest and most rewarding times of our working lives. We spend a lot of time working and need to love what we do and do what we love. In this little booklet, I hope to explore how we can create and maintain these happy and rewarding careers for ourselves.

CHAPTER 1- Why do we work?

"We work to have leisure on which our happiness depends" — *Aristotle.*

A few years ago, I took a group of matriculants to a "Careers Day" at one of our prestigious educational institutions. We spent the day exploring different career options in workshops and discussions with employers, educators, etc. On our way home, we drove past a lady driving a beautiful luxury car and one of the girls pronounced that she had decided that she would like to become an Accountant so that she can drive a beautiful car like that. I was quite surprised at the reason for her decision after all we had learnt during the day and a whole host of questions sprang to mind.

- Does she know what an Accountant really does day to day and how they contribute to the business world and society?
- Does she enjoy accounting at school?
- Do her grades reflect her capability to do this work?

- Does she think that when she becomes an Accountant she will automatically qualify for the lovely car and a big salary to match?
- Will she be happy to work as an Accountant for the rest of her life? etc.

Why exactly is it that as human beings we choose to spend 8 hours of every day of our lives away from our loved ones doing work that sometimes fails to interest or excite us, may be unrewarding and difficult and may even be bad for us. Is it just to earn money to meet our financial needs for survival and leisure and to drive that beautiful car or is there in fact more to it than that?

Work has several purposes, including the more practical reasons like earning enough money to pay for daily expenses, our family's needs and our leisure time. Work also provides people with a feeling of personal purpose and accomplishment, and contributes to developments that benefit communities and societies. Work also helps to accomplish those things that help to improve our lives and provides us opportunities for personal growth.

When we work, we are providing our skills, expertise and knowledge in exchange for a salary and are also contributing to the society we live in. Working gives us a sense of purpose and generally allows people to feel that they are contributing something of value.

"The purpose of work is that work gives us purpose."

When you speak to people who are unemployed the biggest problems that they face are not only linked to the lack of ability to earn an income but also the lack of purpose and direction (no reason to get up and get dressed each day) and the resulting lack of self-esteem.

It stands to reason then that those who are happiest in their work are those who do work that gives them a sense of meaning, purpose and value in their lives. It is however also important to do work that enables us to make the most of our current capabilities and skills.

When we are required to do work that consistently requires us to stretch beyond our current skills and capabilities we feel overwhelmed and can experience anxiety and stress at work, however if we are required to consistently do work that does not stretch our capabilities sufficiently we begin to feel underutilised and wasted.

As humans, we also have a need to grow and develop throughout our lives and our work should therefore also offer us opportunities to develop ourselves in line with our potential over time, either deepening our skills and becoming more specialised or broadening our work base to take on more complexity at work.

We spend a large proportion of our lives working and may as well do something that we are capable of doing and that we enjoy, that gives us a sense of purpose and that adds value for and is also valued by others.

The starting point to finding that perfect job therefore seems to be one of honestly identifying one's current skills and capabilities, establishing what gives you a sense of meaning and purpose in life and then balancing that with what is available in the market and will meet your personal needs in terms of financial rewards and personal growth.

The trend in career development advice is to follow one's passion and the rewards will follow, which is great, but unfortunately real life doesn't always follow this 'fairy-tale' view. E.g. My passion for creativity and art alone is not going to automatically make me an artist who can produce and sell enough art to support myself and my family over the long term. I need to be skilled and capable as an artist and a marketer, I need to be producing something I feel has value and that others will value, I need to consistently maintain a high standard of work and have a positive attitude and I need to be constantly evolving and growing as an artist, etc., etc. to establish a sustainable career in the arts. I do need passion but to sustain a career and achieve excellence, I need far more than just passion. I need to not only do what I love but also, I need to love what I do. Perhaps it's more about being passionate about what we do, rather than simply following our passion.

> "Your work is going to fill a large part of your life, and the only way to be truly satisfied is to do what you believe is great work, and the only way to do great work is to love what you do."
>
> Steve Jobs

WHY WE WORK ....

- To earn money to satisfy our day to day needs and the needs of our family

- To enjoy our leisure time, have nice things, etc.

- To satisfy our human need for purpose and accomplishment

- To have self-esteem and fulfil our potential

- To add value and contribute to the improvement of society and our community

- To fulfil our need for personal growth

WHICH OF THESE REASONS FOR WORKING IS THE MOST IMPORTANT TO YOU?

CHAPTER 2-Identifying your Potential

How do we find out what our potential is, what we enjoy doing most and what our talents, skills, capabilities and strengths are so that we can find this perfect job?

We go back to the philosopher Aristotle again.... Aristotle believed that the universe is in a state of constant motion, always changing, and evolving. However, at the same time, there is one thing that remains a constant in everything—what he called "entelechy" or one's essential potential.

Aristotle believed that everything on the planet possesses its own entelechy, or as he coined it, "having one's end within." Entelechy is a vital force that motivates and guides an organism toward self-fulfilment. We could also see this as our God given potential. The mere stuff or matter is not yet the real thing; it needs a certain form or essence or function to complete it. As an example, if you think of an Oak tree. It starts out its life as a seed or acorn and it grows and develops through various stages and given the right conditions (good soil, enough water, sunlight, etc.) eventually becomes a big majestic oak tree.

That is its essential potential, it will never grow into a rose bush or a tomato plant, no matter what the conditions are. It may not grow into the biggest tree in the forest if the conditions are not suitable but it may also grow more effectively in harsher conditions where it must build resilience as it faces environmental challenges.

According to Aristotle, there is always a reason for everything that happens. Your experiences are designed to shape and define you so that you can grow into the best you possible and fulfil your potential. We could also see this a God's plan or purpose for our lives. Aristotle also said that as humans we have the advantage of conscious insight, i.e. an ability to tap into ourselves and our experiences, both positive and negative and to learn and grow from them. So, the good news then is that if we consistently draw on our conscious insight to understand ourselves and our experiences better and we focus on our end goal or potential we can perhaps have much more fulfilling work lives.

"You do not become good by trying to be good, but by finding the goodness that is already within you." ~Eckhart Tolle

As young adults when we finish our schooling years we are encouraged to find out "what we want to be when we grow up". We go to career counselling and we go through tests to identify our interests and strengths and weaknesses and match those with possible careers. While this is useful in that it gives us an opportunity to reflect on our interests and strengths at that time and gain some insight into possible career choices, it is important to remember that that is only the starting point. A career can span an entire lifetime and over that period one's interests, capabilities, thinking style, circumstances, values, etc. are bound to change. Conscious insight is therefore something that is gained as one develops over a lifetime and you could conceivably reinvent your career several times as you go through life. To stay happy and fulfilled at work, you therefore need to regularly re-evaluate your progress towards your potential.

"Many people use the word potential yet few realize that your potential defines who you are, what you can excel at, and what is possible for you to become."

Take a few moments to ask yourself these questions. Be honest, realistic and specific and write the answers down....

- Do I know what my potential is?
- Do I know what I could be good at?
- What do I excel at?
- What can I usually do better than others can?
- What could I excel at with the right resources and training?
- What is possible for me?
- What do I dream of being or becoming?
- Who do I want to work with?
- What place of work would inspire me most?
- What tasks or activities am I great at?
- What kind of life do I want to manifest? How can I contribute value to society and my community?

I always knew I wanted to become somebody when I grew up. Now I realize I should have been more specific. - Lily Tomlin

If I were to wish for anything, I should not wish for wealth and power, but for the passionate sense of the potential, for the eye which, ever young and ardent, sees the possible. What wine is so sparkling, so fragrant, so intoxicating, as possibility!

- Soren Kierkegaard

IT'S NEVER TOO LATE TO BE WHAT YOU MIGHT HAVE BEEN.
- GEORGE ELLIOT

Our potential be the sum of our unique and individual talents, skills and knowledge, our personality characteristics, competencies and behaviour, attitude, self-belief, will power, drive, circumstances, relationships, opportunities, etc. Achieving your own personal potential therefore means making the most of these aspects over a lifetime. Honestly identifying areas of strength that one can build on and areas that may need improvement to move closer to one's best potential becomes important in this process of gaining self-insight.

There are many ways of gaining these personal insights, including:

- Self-exploration, Journaling, etc.
- Assessment of personality (MBTI, 16PF, etc.), values, interests, and other psychometrics
- Listening to feedback from others (360 degree processes)
- Behavioural and competency assessments
- Career Coaching Processes
- Appreciative Conversations around potential (CPA, IRIS, etc.)

> **If a man has talent and can't use it, he's failed. If he uses only half of it, he has partly failed. If he uses the whole of it, he has succeeded, and won a satisfaction and triumph few men ever know.**
> **– Thomas Wolfe**

Self-insight can be gained at various times in one's life. Some people have a clear idea of what their potential is while they are young or still at school, others develop self-insight as they grow through various work and life experiences and some sadly reach the end of their work lives never really understanding their full essential potential. It is important though to remember that at whatever point self-insight comes, it can still be transformed into self-realisation so it's worth pursuing throughout your life.

TIPS FOR GAINING INSIGHT INTO YOUR MOST FULFILLING WORK ROLE

- Get to know yourself better and to understand your unique needs, strengths and talents and try to match your job with your capabilities.
- Do work that gives you a feeling of satisfaction and confidence.
- Find your "Flow" i.e. those activities where time passes and you are so engrossed in what you are doing that you hardly notice it.
- Love what you do and try to do work that fulfils your potential and purpose.
- We usually describe ourselves by referring to what we do. Try to do work that you wold proudly define yourself by.
- Believe in yourself and what is possible.

CHAPTER 3-Marketing Yourself

Once you understand yourself and your potential you can start planning how to go about marketing yourself effectively. Just like any marketing campaign your aim is to find the best buyers for your product -yourself and your talents. You want to ultimately find someone who will be a suitable match for you and your skills and potential and who is also willing to provide you a salary in exchange for your contribution. You need to present yourself in the best light to do this but you also need to understand who your potential employers are and what they need to ensure a good match.

The starting point of any good marketing campaign is to gain insight into your WWHP, i.e.

W WHO- You need to know who your potential customers are and what they are trying to achieve or what their needs are but in the case of marketing yourself you also must understand who you are and what skills, abilities and potential you can offer a potential buyer/employer.

W WHERE- You need to know where to go to, to find potential employers that you would ideally like to work for. E.g. Career guidance centres at educational institutions, career expo's, Industry players and leaders, internet e.g.

linked-in, market research, local or global newspapers, journals, your own business networks, etc.

H HOW- You need to put together a clear plan of how to sell yourself and your skills effectively and identify the various platforms that can be used to find what you need. e.g. Social Media, Advertisements, Word of Mouth, Networks, Letters of application, Agents, sending out CV's, etc. Make sure that any information about yourself on various social network platforms is positive and consistent.

P PROFIT- What you and your potential employer stand to gain, i.e. financial rewards, job satisfaction, a solid loyal and happy employee, good decision making, value contribution to the organisation, benefits, challenging interesting work, a contribution to society and the community, etc. This also needs to be balanced with the cost of achieving this. Financial cost. cost to your family, cost to your own health and well- being, etc.

DRAW UP A PLAN TO MARKET YOURSELF AND TRY TO BE SPECIFIC ABOUT EACH OF THESE ASPECTS WHO, WHERE, HOW AND PROFIT

One of the most important documents in this marketing process is your CV or resume. Many organisations require a CV as a starting point in getting to know who you are and what you can offer their business. Your CV therefore needs to reflect who you are, your potential and what you want to achieve at work, as well as what you hope to contribute. This is a very important document and can make or break your chances of getting a foot in the door or an invitation to that all-important interview where you can really sell yourself and your skills.

What should your CV include?

- Start with a summary of your personal details, i.e. Name, age and date of birth, location, email details and contact telephone numbers, etc.

- Provide a short summary of your most important purpose at work.

- Provide full and accurate information on your educational qualifications.

- Provide a short summary of positions held throughout your career to date, starting with your most recent position.

Provide information around professional memberships and positions held in social and professional bodies outside of your immediate work environment that could be relevant to your work.

Provide at least 3 references with current contact details, who can be contacted and know you have named them as references.

TIPS FOR WRITING A GOOD CV

It is important that your CV should be brief, current and to the point. Bear in mind that employers have many CV's crossing their desks each day and that they don't have the time to read through reams of detail.

Your CV should be neatly presented and checked and rechecked for spelling and grammar errors.

Your CV should always be accompanied by a short personalised letter introducing yourself and stating the purpose of your interest in the company or the specific position you may be interested in.

Your CV should be easy to read and organised in such a way that the important aspects of who you are and what you would like to contribute are easy to pick up in a few minutes.

Avoid using too many graphics and too much colour. Less is always more. Stick to a simple and readable font.

You should not include a photograph of yourself unless asked to do so and if you do have to include a photograph it should be a professional head and shoulders shot against a neutral background.

Your CV is not the place to boast about your abilities and should only cover the most important facts about what you can do for the employer.

You should not include reasons why you left your previous employers. This can be discussed in an interview.

Don't include details about your current salary or required salary, those are confidential and can be discussed in an interview if necessary.

Don't include personal details around race, religion, etc.

Make sure your references know you are using their names and ensure that their contact details are current. Choose references that know you well and can vouch for your good character.

CHAPTER 4-The Interview

So, you have now marketed yourself effectively and your CV has caught the attention of your chosen prospective employers. You have been invited to that all-important interview and now you really must pull out all the stops to impress and present yourself as a valuable asset to an organisation. This is your opportunity to shine and to convince others of your worth but don't forget that the interview is a two-way conversation where the employer also needs to convince you that this is where you would love to work. This is where you can grow and work towards reaching your best potential.

Let's face it, interviews can be daunting and most of us would rather avoid them but they are necessary to enable the employer to get to know who you are and what you can really offer as well as for you to get to know more about what the employer can offer you. The important thing is to be well prepared. Going into the interviewed with some knowledge of the company and who will be interviewing you and with a positive and confident attitude always helps to reduce much of the tension.

It would be wonderful if we knew exactly what the interviewer would be asking us but unfortunately that is often not possible. There are however a few general questions that come up in most interviews and being prepared for them goes a long way to your interview being successful.

Common Interview questions

Tell me a little about yourself?
How did you hear about this position?
What do you know about our business?
Why would you like to work for this company?
What can you offer this company and what do you expect this company to do for you?
Why do you think we should hire you?
What are your career goals and future plans?
What professional strengths can you bring to this business?
Do you believe that you have any weaknesses that could affect your performance at work?
What has been your best achievement at work?
Tell me about a major challenge or decision that you have faced at work and how you dealt with it?
What projects have you been involved in ant work and what role did you play in them?
Have you had the opportunity to lead or manage a team at work and what did the team look like?
How do you feel about rules at work?
How do you spend your time away from work?
What are your life dreams?
What are your expectations in terms of salary?
How would you think others would generally describe you?
Who has had the most major impact on your career to date?
Why do you want to change careers?
Do you have any questions for me?

Sitting down beforehand and thinking about and perhaps even mentally preparing answers to these types of questions enables you to be more relaxed and confident during the interview process. (Don't take crib notes with you though as you would then just come across as contrived and less than genuine).

When asked questions about yourself avoid the trap of going through your entire career history. Rather select a few important and compelling aspects of your career that would be pertinent to the position on offer and give a concise and genuine account of who you are and how your previous experience can benefit you in the role.

When asked questions about the company use the opportunity to connect with what the company does and how that intersects with your own passion and purpose. They don't want to know how many facts you have at your fingertips about the company, but they do want to know whether you care about what the company is trying to achieve. Show that you understand the company's goals, e.g." I really appreciate that this company is wanting to......."

It's important to show passion and enthusiasm for what you can do and the value you can add to the company. If you are not able to do this perhaps you should think about applying for a position in a different work environment.

Why do you think we should hire you? can be one of the more intimidating questions that employers often ask and while it can be a bit awkward to answer it does give you an opportunity to sell yourself. You can use it as an opening to highlight what you can offer in terms of skills and competencies, what you can deliver in terms of results and how you will fit in with the team and business culture.

Equally questions around your strengths and weaknesses also open this discussion. You should focus on strengths that have a direct bearing on the role and required business outcomes and on weaknesses that you are aware of and are working on to improve. Avoid being boastful and arrogant, i.e. listing all your best traits and denying any weak areas.

When asked questions about assignments you have done in the past, use the STAR method to concisely describe the project in a **specific** manner, focusing on **tasks** that you did, **actions** that were required and the **results**. e.g. While working at the bank, I was involved in a project that ran over two years to develop a new system for data capture in Human Resources. I was responsible for sourcing the contractors and managing the process of designing and then writing the code for the system as well as all the testing. The system was implemented ahead of time within 18 months and has been a great success having subsequently been rolled out to other divisions in the organisation.

When faced with questions around the rules and ethics at work, an honest approach is always the best approach. Don't try to impress the interviewer by saying what you think they want to hear. If your views are not aligned with the organisational values, you are simply going to have a hard time working there and should perhaps seek another option. There is only one right answer to these kinds of questions and that is what is right for you, so just be straightforward in saying what you really think. I once worked for an organisation where it was initially expected (as an unwritten rule) of us to stay after hours and have a drink with our clients to build relationships. This just did not gel with my values and I had to be clear and upfront about it or it would have caused me a lot of unhappy evenings away from my family. I then looked at other ways to build client relationships that did not involve evenings spent in the pub and before long the unwritten rule was a thing of the past.

When asked questions about your future goals and career dreams, you should also take the honest approach and highlight what you would see as being realistic and achievable goals. It is important to be seen to have passion for what you do and some ambition but try to focus on what can be achieved within the company in the foreseeable future and mention your overall longer term passion briefly. Also, perhaps mention what you are doing to work towards these goals. e.g. I think I could possibly work effectively as an Operations Manager within the next 5 years and I have thought of registering for a Management Development Programme to help me to achieve that. Perhaps before I retire, it would be nice to contribute to the company at a General Management level or have an opportunity to run a business. Again, don't try to second guess what they might want you to say.... just be yourself. They want to know whether you are driven to add value to their business in the longer term and the best place to add value is where you are comfortable with the challenges you face. They also want to know whether the business can accommodate your goals and aspirations and your potential growth.

Discussions around salary requirements can also be tricky. Do your research beforehand so that you have an idea of what can be expected realistically, given the market, the role and your own skills, qualifications, experience, etc. Have a number in mind before you negotiate so that you don't undersell yourself but also be open to looking at what the employer can offer given the market, business environment, economic climate, etc. You want to reach a "win, win" where you are remunerated in line with your skills but you don't want to completely exclude yourself from the market with demands that are too high for the business to handle. You want to make it clear that you know how valuable your skills are but also that you really do want the job and are willing to negotiate to some extent.

Finally, the most difficult questions in an interview are those relating to your career moves and the reason you are wanting to make a change. Again, honesty is the best policy.

Sometimes your interviewer may ask a few fun questions as well. e.g. What animal would you think best describes you? or If you won the lottery, what would you do? Have fun with these to show that you have a creative mind.

So now you are prepared for any question that can be thrown at you and the big day arrives. You want to put your best foot forward and impress...maybe a few pointers on Interview Etiquette may be useful. The most important things are to be neatly presented, on time, well-prepared and informed. You should be confident, keen and passionate and present yourself in the best way possible. You could see the interview as a sales pitch where you are the product but remember that it is a two-way exchange and it is also an opportunity to see whether the position is the best fit for you now. Be open, enthusiastic, positive and flexible and you should have an enjoyable interview experience but most of all BE YOURSELF.

After the interview, also remember that the communication does not end here. A friendly thank-you email to your interviewer for his/her time and interest in you as well as any "next steps" should follow. Commit to following up but don't overdo it by phoning the interviewer every day for feedback.

INTERVIEW ETIQUETTE 101

Make sure you have diarised the place, person's name, date and time correctly.

Dress appropriately for the Interview- Ensure that your appearance is professional, neat, clean and acceptable for the given work context. (First Impressions mean a lot).

Make sure that you arrive at least 15 minutes before the interview time to give yourself an opportunity to relax, freshen up and be at your best and wait in the reception area until you are called in for the interview.

Don't take food or drink into the interview and don't chew gum.

Greet your interviewer courteously and thank him/ her for the opportunity to interview for the position.

Smile your way to success and be polite.

Be friendly, relaxed and confident but avoid a casual or overly arrogant approach- "Confidence isn't about thinking you are better than everyone else, it's about believing that you don' t have to compare yourself to others."

Use your interviewer's (correct) name during the discussion.

Comfortable eye contact is so important.

Be aware and sensitive to body language- your own and that of the interviewer.

Don't appear desperate but show that you are keen and passionate.

Don't be negative about your current or previous employers.

Be prepared and Informed

CHAPTER 5- Maintaining the Passion

After the interview process, there can usually only be a few possible outcomes, rejection, further discussions, testing, etc., or what we all want - that all important job offer with a contract on the table.

If you are rejected it is important to get feedback so that you have a clear idea of where you may fall short or where there was a mismatch between you and the company. This helps you to focus on how to change your approach in future or what you need to do to improve. Try as far as possible to remove emotion from the equation and be objective. You should probably get feedback from the recruiter or the individual who conducted the interview and usually the best approach would be to send an email so that you are not putting them on the spot. Be open and gracious about the feedback. Get back out there and try again. If necessary, continue doing what you are doing or find an alternative until you find the job of your dreams. You must be realistic and continue "bringing in the bacon" until the job you love is available for you.

You may also be asked to go through further discussions, psychometric tests, etc. See this as a positive sign and although you may not yet have a foot in the door, these are also opportunities for you to learn more about yourself and the company, so that a more relevant and fruitful decision can be made.

"DON'T LET REJECTIONS WEIGH YOU DOWN. PUT THEM UNDER YOUR FEET AND USE THEM AS STEPPING STONES."

HOW TO STAY MOTIVATED

- **Take one day at a time.**
- **Surround yourself with positivity.**
- **Believe in yourself and your strengths.**
- **Try not to be discouraged by rejection.**
- **Accept that disappointment is sometimes part of the process.**
- **Set realistic goals.**
- **Don't give up.**
- **Be kind to yourself and remember your perfect job is out there. While you are still searching, do something positive to use your time and keep yourself motivated and develop your skills, e.g. do a course.**
- **Seek every opportunity you can to learn, grow and achieve your best.**

What we all want is to find that perfect job and have a contract on the table. This however is only the beginning of the journey. We need to continue to live our passion and achieve fulfilment through the work that we have been provided so that we too can say, "I LOVE MY JOB". We need to do what we love and love what we do to continue achieving our best potential

The most important factors for success in finding that perfect role for you are a positive attitude, passion and enthusiasm balanced with information, knowledge, preparation and realistic self-insight.

www.ingramcontent.com/pod-product-compliance
Lightning Source LLC
Chambersburg PA
CBHW041211180526
45172CB00006B/1232